When Your Wife Gets on Your Nerves —or Worse

52 Verses to Bolster You

Mary Stone

When Your Wife Gets on Your Nerves—or Worse

Also by Mary Stone

Non-Fiction

Run in the Path of Peace—the Secret of Being Content No Matter What

When Your Husband is a Christian—But Doesn't Always Act Like One; 52 Verses to Bolster You

When You Have an Unsaved Loved One; 52 Devotions to Give You Hope

Fiction

In BeTWEEN TROUBLE

Table of Contents

When Your Wife Gets on Your Nerves —or Worse

52 Verses to Bolster You

Bolster: A structural component designed to eliminate friction or provide support or bearing.

"Your statutes are my delight; they are my counselors."
—Psalm 119:24

This book is not about your wife but about *you* and how you can be victorious in your walk with the Lord and in your marriage, despite conflicts and circumstances you find distressing and/or hurtful.

Why 52 verses?

When you focus on one verse throughout the week, and others every week of the year, you store these verses in your mind and heart. By repeating, you go deep within scripture, mining the treasures God has for you in those portions of His Word.

The result? You will be encouraged, strengthened, and armed to intercede for your loved one.

Although each of the following messages begins with something your wife does or doesn't do, this book is about *you* and how you can use each situation to grow in Christ. Some circumstances will apply to you, others won't. Those that don't, offer you an opportunity to praise God that your wife doesn't behave in that manner, and the opportunity to lift up in prayer your brothers in Christ who do live in those conditions. However, the more of these 52 instances you encounter, the more occasion you have for spiritual growth.

The scriptures given for each situation are not exclusive but rather interchangeable with other circumstances. So if one week's issue doesn't apply to you, claim the verse to help you thrive in Christ, regardless.

As well, this book is not about how to have a perfect marriage but rather how to act as a man of God within an imperfect marriage. The reality is, not one of us is perfect. We all have our faults. As you move through each message, ask yourself, "Am I guilty of this?" Ask God to shine a light upon your behaviors and thoughts. Herein is more room for growth.

Some of the issues addressed may seem similar, yet they are not exactly the same. Each deserves its own focus. As well, you will find the theme of communicating with your spouse and seeking the Lord thread throughout the weeks. Consistently applying these approaches will empower you to be victorious.

While communication with your spouse is vital, another reality is, not everyone is willing to discuss issues. You can only do what you can do—be open and non-critical in your approach to invite your wife to converse.

As a marriage and individual counselor for many years—having the opportunity to work with those from various ages, backgrounds, cultures, and faiths—I encountered the issues you will read in the following 52 weeks of verses. These matters are best addressed between partners who are devoted to Christ. Even then, although both are saved, not everyone responds to making changes in a godly way. It is up to *you* to respond in the way God leads as you entrust your wife to Him, for only He can change any of us.

These pages speak of some behaviors which are sin. However, the majority of these spousal behaviors fall into a category of irksome, or under behaviors that are less than honoring to the marriage relationship. That said, the intent of each weekly message is not to criticize or accuse your wife but to provide a way for you to persevere in the circumstances and grow in Christ.

As you move through each page, I encourage you to utilize . . .

7 Essential Elements

1. Pray for your wife and yourself.

2. Ask God to help you see the situation through His eyes.

3. Ask God for wisdom.

4. Converse with your wife.

5. Accept that you cannot change your spouse—only yourself.

6. Pick your battles.

7. Forgive and continue to forgive.

"I will praise the LORD, who counsels me; even at night my heart instructs me. I keep my eyes always on the LORD. With him at my right hand, I will not be shaken."—Psalm 16:7-8

Week 1   When your wife does not embrace the fullness of Ephesians 5:22, instructing her to submit to you . . .

"Husbands, love your wives, as Christ also loved the church and gave himself up for her."—Ephesians 5:25

Do you consider your wife as a gift from God? Whether you answer yes or no, you are in a relationship ordained by God. Consider how Jesus loves both you and your spouse, and how His love is not conditional on acceptance of your behaviors, your "performance" as a Christian.

To love your wife unconditionally requires you to accept her as Jesus sees her—with faults as she grows in her faith. This may not always be easy, especially when you take your role as head of the household seriously. You want to protect, to provide, to set an example of Christlikeness. You want to hold yourself to the highest standard so you can be a leader in this marriage.

Do you find yourself frustrated when your wife somehow minimizes or thwarts your leadership? If so, consider how Jesus must feel when you fail to follow Him.

So, how do you follow Christ when your bride doesn't submit to you?

The answer is, *love her as Jesus loves you. Pray for your beloved. Lift her up. Treat her with respect. Adore and cherish her as she is. Set a shining example of loving and submitting to Christ.*

Which Bible verses can help you do these things?

Week 1 Reflections

Day 1: This week's verse in full, or a portion thereof:

____

____

____

Day 2: This verse empowers me to:

____

____

____

Day 3: My response to the entreaty at the end of the message:

____

____

____

Day 4: What I most appreciate about my wife this day/week:

____

____

____

Day 5: Prayer:

____

____

____

Week 2   When your wife tries to change you . . .

". . . Strive for full restoration, encourage one another, be of one mind, live in peace. And the God of love and peace will be with you."—2 Corinthians 13:11

Most likely, you haven't changed much since you first met your wife, so perhaps you are nonplussed as to why now she is dissatisfied with the way you are or do things. This is great fodder for conversation—when approached gently and sincerely. And of course, preceded by prayer.

E.g. "Dear, please help me understand what is different about me than when we dated. During that time, it didn't seem as if you disliked certain things about me. Or that what I do now bothered you then."

It is vital for you to listen with an open mind and heart. Acknowledge what your wife says. Then discuss if your behaviors need to change, or whether she could accept you as you are—faults and all.

If this discussion does not go well, it is time to attend a Christian marriage retreat or seek couples counseling. Either of these options can strengthen your relationship. The important thing is to not put off coming to a full restoration as Paul wrote about in 2 Corinthians 13. He penned these verses when he discovered the Corinth church was wrestling with issues. Paul encouraged this body of believers to preserve the unity among them.

How can you and your wife be of one mind and live in peace?

Week 2 Reflections

Day 1: This week's verse in full, or a portion thereof:

____

____

____

Day 2: This verse empowers me to:

____

____

____

Day 3: My response to the entreaty at the end of the message:

____

____

____

Day 4: What I most appreciate about my wife this day/week:

____

____

____

Day 5: Prayer:

____

____

____

Week 3   When your wife gets defensive or puts up a wall when you try to discuss things with her . . .

"Now go; I will help you speak and will teach you what to say."—Exodus 4:12

When God spoke these words to Moses, Moses was having a difficult time getting the Israelites to listen to him. Your circumstances are different than Moses', but you both serve(d) the same God—Who is the same yesterday, today, and forever.

The Lord had chosen Moses to lead, just as He has appointed you to lead in your home.

In both instances, the Heavenly Father did not and does not appoint to then simply leave you on your own.

When you accepted Jesus as your Savior, the Holy Spirit took up residence inside you as promised in 1 Corinthians 6:19. This is the same Spirit spoken of in Isaiah 11:2: "The Spirit of the LORD will rest on him [Jesus]—the Spirit of wisdom and of understanding, the Spirit of counsel and of might, the Spirit of the knowledge and fear of the LORD."

How awesome is it to have this Counselor at the ready, waiting for you to ask for guidance. He knows you and your wife intimately. Therefore, the wisdom and understanding He will provide will enable you to talk with your betrothed in a manner pleasing to Him and acceptable to your wife.

As you are quiet before the Lord, beseeching Him for guidance, and waiting for His leading, what is He saying to you?

Week 3 Reflections

Day 1: This week's verse in full, or a portion thereof:

Day 2: This verse empowers me to:

Day 3: My response to the entreaty at the end of the message:

Day 4: What I most appreciate about my wife this day/week:

Day 5: Prayer:

13

Week 4 When your wife devotes more of herself to her profession than she does to you . . .

"But he said to me, 'My grace is sufficient for you, for my power is made perfect in weakness.' Therefore I will boast all the more gladly about my weaknesses, so that Christ's power may rest on me."—2 Corinthians 12:9-10

When a wife spends more time and/or interest in her profession than in her marriage, sometimes a husband feels hurt, abandoned, or emasculated. (Emasculated in this sense meaning weakened or undermined.) Do you experience any of these feelings?

If so, you likely miss the emotional and physical intimacy you once shared with your bride. Do you then sense you are "not enough" for her since she finds fulfillment in her career?

This is when the enemy swoops in to encourage you to weaken your resolve to strengthen your relationship with the woman you love.

Mercifully, God has a better plan. As God told Paul when he felt weakened by circumstances, His grace was sufficient. This word comes from the Greek word *arkeo*, which means to give protection, power, and help.

The Lord's grace is exactly what you can call upon now so that Christ's power and strength will rest on you as you determine to woo your beloved back into your arms—not away from her job— but that once again you would be her heart's earthly desire.

Even though you may find it strange to gladly boast about your weaknesses, will you do so for Christ's power to rest on you?

Week 4 Reflections

Day 1: This week's verse in full, or a portion thereof:

____

____

____

Day 2: This verse empowers me to:

____

____

____

Day 3: My response to the entreaty at the end of the message:

____

____

____

Day 4: What I most appreciate about my wife this day/week:

____

____

____

Day 5: Prayer:

____

____

____

Week 5   When your wife shares your marriage issues with her mother . . .

"Let the words of my mouth and the meditation of my heart be acceptable in your sight O LORD, my rock and my redeemer."
—Psalm 19:14

David offered this heartfelt prayer to God as he sought a right relationship with Him. With the words of this verse, he surrenders to the Lord's leading, while praising Him as his rock and redeemer.

While the words spilling from your spouse's mouth to her mother's ears are not acceptable to you, you cannot control what your wife says or does. You only have jurisdiction over yourself.

So, step back and let God work in your wife's heart. He is better at convicting than you ever could be . . . with more promising results. Be certain to make room for the Lord to fight on your behalf—because He is your rock and your redeemer.

Ask God to reveal if there is something keeping your loved one from opening up to you, so she instead turns to her mother. On the other hand, perhaps it is nothing you are doing but rather that your wife has always had a close relationship with her mother and fears losing that.

Consider what words and thoughts in this situation would be acceptable to your Heavenly Father. What words spoken to and thoughts of your wife would be pleasing to her?

What will you ask God for regarding your wife, yourself, and your mother-in-law?

19

Week 5 Reflections

Day 1: This week's verse in full, or a portion thereof:

____

____

____

Day 2: This verse empowers me to:

____

____

____

Day 3: My response to the entreaty at the end of the message:

____

____

____

Day 4: What I most appreciate about my wife this day/week:

____

____

____

Day 5: Prayer:

____

____

21

Week 6   When your wife acts like her mother . . .

*"What shall I return to the LORD for all his goodness to me? . . .
I will fulfill my vows to the LORD in the presence of all his
people."*—Psalm 116:12, 14

When you looked your bride in the eyes at the altar and took your vows before God "to love and to cherish from this day forward," most likely you did not see her mother standing before you. Yet now your mother-in-law has somehow invaded your home via your wife's body.

Maybe you like your mother-in-law . . . or not. Either way, it is difficult to be intimate, whether in conversation or otherwise, with the woman you love when she reminds you of her mom.

When disagreements arise between you and your wife, the enemy shouts in your ear for you to proclaim, "You're just like your mother!" This is a sure-fire fight starter. Even if your mother-in-law is a wonderful Christian woman, this accusation is belittling and fraught with contempt.

The only way out of this allegation is for you to apologize. Follow this with speaking well of your mother-in-law and recognizing what you appreciate about her. Once the heat of the moment has passed, pray together, then try to get to the heart of the real issue.

Ask your wife what she needs from you. Listen and repeat this to her to make sure you heard correctly. Praise God for her honesty while silently asking Him to help you with this.

What do you need to do to fulfill your marriage vows today, tomorrow, and the next day?

23

Week 6 Reflections

Day 1: This week's verse in full, or a portion thereof:

____

____

____

Day 2: This verse empowers me to:

____

____

____

Day 3: My response to the entreaty at the end of the message:

____

____

____

Day 4: What I most appreciate about my wife this day/week:

____

____

____

Day 5: Prayer:

____

____

____

25

Week 7   When your wife lets the household chores go . . .

"Husbands, love your wives just as Christ loved the church and gave himself up for her to make her holy, cleansing her by the washing with water through the word, and to present her to himself as a radiant church, without stain or wrinkle or any other blemish, but holy and blameless."—Ephesians 5:26-27

You come home from work to relax in your castle. Yet when you enter the house you are met with dirty dishes, unwashed clothes, and junk piled on your favorite chair. This compounds the jumble in your mind of things gone wrong on your job. You want to veg out, but it is difficult to rest and rejuvenate when everything around you is in disarray.

If your wife works outside the home, you likely understand how things have gotten to this point, and probably pitch in to share the load at home.

However, if your wife stays home and your children are in school, it is hard to envision how she spends her day. Perhaps she is depressed or unmotivated because she doesn't find fulfillment in being a housewife. If so, this is a perfect opportunity to apply Ephesians 5:26-27.

Even though your house isn't clean, is stained, and clothes are wrinkled, you can cleanse *her* by washing her with the Word.

What verses will you share with your beloved, not to convict, but to encourage and strengthen her?

E.g. God delights in her—Isaiah 62: 4; She is God's Masterpiece—Ephesians 2:10

Week 7 Reflections

Day 1: This week's verse in full, or a portion thereof:

____

____

____

Day 2: This verse empowers me to:

____

____

____

Day 3: My response to the entreaty at the end of the message:

____

____

____

Day 4: What I most appreciate about my wife this day/week:

____

____

____

Day 5: Prayer:

____

____

____

Week 8   When your wife withdraws and won't tell you what is wrong . . .

"There is a time for everything . . . a time to embrace and a time to refrain from embracing . . . a time to be silent and a time to speak . . . ." —Ecclesiastes 3:1, 5, 7

It is challenging to help the one you love when she won't let you. It is normal to jump to conclusions as to what might be bothering her. It is hazardous to assume you know why she won't open up.

It is also harmful to your relationship to respond in silence as well. Share with her your desire to discuss things because it hurts you to see her hurting. Then listen. Be careful not to push, prod, or hurry your wife. For indeed, there is a time to be silent and a time to speak. Perhaps she is processing emotions, thoughts, and wants to get things straight in her mind before she invites you in.

If the time for her to speak is not in this moment, let her know you will wait. While doing so allows you time to go to the Lord with this situation. Draw near to Him, present your desire to help your wife, then leave it in His hands . . . and be silent while you listen.

Communication is a two-way journey, involving speaking and listening, whether with your loved one or with your Heavenly Father.

Will you listen to the Holy Spirit as you speak words of love and encouragement to your wife?

Week 8 Reflections

Day 1: This week's verse in full, or a portion thereof:

____

____

____

Day 2: This verse empowers me to:

____

____

____

Day 3: My response to the entreaty at the end of the message:

____

____

____

Day 4: What I most appreciate about my wife this day/week:

____

____

____

Day 5: Prayer:

____

____

____

Week 9   When your wife doesn't have any outside interests or hobbies . . .

"Therefore encourage one another and build each other up, just as in fact you are doing." —1 Thessalonians 5:11

Does it seem your wife has made you her whole world? If so, you likely feel the burden of what this requires of you. It is just a matter of time before you let her down—not long before you are not sufficient to provide all that she expects, or wants. (Something God never intended for either of you in the first place.)

These circumstances can also affect your freedom to pursue your own interests. If this happens, before you know it, most likely you will feel resentment. The enemy will take this and fan into flames your anger and bitterness toward your wife. Hopefully, you are not there yet. But even if you have experienced these emotions, it is never too late for God to deliver you from the enemy's talons.

Ask God to help you and your wife recall her interests and hobbies before you married. Ask the Lord to reignite these passions within her. Request of the Lord that He help your wife identify new pursuits. Ask your Heavenly Father to show you how you can encourage her to pursue these enjoyable ventures.

As your loved one rediscovers these endeavors, build her up by telling her how much it delights you to see her enjoying herself.

How can you encourage your wife's heart and spirit today?
How is the Lord leading you to build her up?

Week 9 Reflections

Day 1: This week's verse in full, or a portion thereof:

____

____

____

Day 2: This verse empowers me to:

____

____

____

Day 3: My response to the entreaty at the end of the message:

____

____

____

Day 4: What I most appreciate about my wife this day/week:

____

____

____

Day 5: Prayer:

____

____

____

Week 10   When your wife resents the time you spend on your hobbies or with your friends . . .

". . . this is what he [the LORD] requires of you: to do what is right, to love mercy, and to walk humbly with your God."—
Micah 6:8

This situation may or may not be related to the previous week's matter—when your wife has no interests outside the home. Regardless, it is important for you to treat each concern separately, even if your wife connects the two.

The thing is, you have no control over what your wife thinks or feels. You may be able to enlighten, encourage, and otherwise help her see things differently, but ultimately you are powerless to make her do or believe anything. Not that you would want to, for that would make you a tyrant.

Considering that, what is left to do?

Micah clearly spells it out in chapter six, verse eight—the Lord requires you to do what is right, love mercy, and walk humbly with God.

What is the right thing to do when your wife is openly resentful over the time you devote to your hobbies or friends? Would God want you to capitulate and give these up? Pray about it, and don't be surprised when He leads you to an alternate solution.

What mercy is required of you toward your wife in this situation? Ask God to show you.

How can you walk humbly (respectfully) with the Lord in this situation?

What is your Father in Heaven revealing to you regarding these questions?

Week 10 Reflections

Day 1: This week's verse in full, or a portion thereof:

____

____

____

Day 2: This verse empowers me to:

____

____

____

Day 3: My response to the entreaty at the end of the message:

____

____

____

Day 4: What I most appreciate about my wife this day/week:

____

____

____

Day 5: Prayer:

____

____

____

Week 11   When your wife has to have the last word . . .

"To answer before listening—that is folly and shame."
—Proverbs 18:13

Usually when one insists on having the last word it is because she doesn't feel heard, understood, or validated.

Examine yourself, your tone of voice, and your words. Ask God to reveal if there is anything in these you would find offensive if your wife, or anyone else, spoke to you this way.

In discussions with your spouse, are you insistent on getting your point across? Even more than that, are you determined to get her to agree with you? Do you interrupt her? Do you talk over her? Do you raise your voice? Before you answer these questions, pause to ask God to help you see what is in your heart and to help you recognize your behaviors.

Psalm 119:130 says the unfolding of God's words gives light and understanding.

Praise Him! When you access scripture, not only will you clearly see your part in the disconcerting situation when your wife has to have the last word, but you will understand why as well.

How empowering this is! Indeed it will help you listen to your beloved and avoid folly and shame all at the same time.

That is easier said than done when in the heat of an argument. Therefore, prior to entering a discussion, pause to pray and call up memorized verses to help you listen and understand your wife.

What Bible verses will you memorize even now to draw from when you need them?

Week 11 Reflections

Day 1: This week's verse in full, or a portion thereof:

____

____

____

Day 2: This verse empowers me to:

____

____

____

Day 3: My response to the entreaty at the end of the message:

____

____

____

Day 4: What I most appreciate about my wife this day/week:

____

____

____

Day 5: Prayer:

____

____

____

41

Week 12   When your wife picks arguments for no apparent reason . . .

"If it is possible, as far as it depends on you, live at peace with everyone."—Romans 12:18

When your wife starts an argument you didn't see coming, does it seem you've been ambushed at the pass? Especially when you see no grounds for a dispute. The worst part is— whether you refuse to engage, or try to reason things out—you are often in a no-win situation. Which might be why the Bible states *"If it is possible, as far as it depends on you,* live at peace with everyone."

So, what do you do to be the peacemaker? Consider these following characteristics of a peacemaker: One who is:

- Patient
- Established in truth
- Kind
- Calm
- Surrendered to God's leading through the Holy Spirit
    - This is perhaps the most vital, as the Holy Spirit knows the truth of the matter and intimately knows both you and your wife. He will impart to you words of wisdom and guidance.

Ask God for His patience and kindness to flow through you . . . for the Spirit of Truth . . . for Him to not only calm your body, soul, and spirit, but to calm the tempest in the home. And most of all, surrender yourself and this situation to the Holy Spirit who is alive and active inside you.

Week 12 Reflections

Day 1: This week's verse in full, or a portion thereof:

____

____

____

Day 2: This verse empowers me to:

____

____

____

Day 3: My response to the entreaty at the end of the message:

____

____

____

Day 4: What I most appreciate about my wife this day/week:

____

____

____

Day 5: Prayer:

____

____

45

Week 13   When your wife criticizes much of what you do . . .

"Do not take revenge, my dear friends, but leave room for God's wrath, for it is written: 'It is mine to avenge; I will repay,' says the Lord. On the contrary: 'If your enemy is hungry, feed him; if he is thirsty, give him something to drink.'"—Romans 12:19-20

It is human nature to counterattack when being attacked. In fact, the enemy amps a person up to do just that. One might say the devil orchestrates fights within a marriage. A whisper here in the ears of God's faithful servants . . . "He never does things right." "He never cleans up after himself." . . . a whisper there . . . "Well she's one to talk. She squeezes the toothpaste in the middle and gets gunk all over the bathroom counter." "She never puts laundry away until it piles up." . . . and soon Satan gains ground to destroy what God has joined together.

These are the little foxes that spoil the vines as referred to in Solomon 2:15, where it speaks of a romance preparing to bear fruit. Foxes are symbolic of potential threats to the relationship. It's the little things that can spoil the love between you and your wife.

Pause to consider what your wife needs—what is she hungry for? What does she thirst for? Ask her these questions when you can both calmly decipher what is going on during times of criticism.

How does God's presence help you accept your wife—flaws and all?

47

Week 13 Reflections

Day 1: This week's verse in full, or a portion thereof:

____

____

____

Day 2: This verse empowers me to:

____

____

____

Day 3: My response to the entreaty at the end of the message:

____

____

____

Day 4: What I most appreciate about my wife this day/week:

____

____

____

Day 5: Prayer:

____

____

____

49

Week 14   When your wife has stopped caring about her personal appearance . . .

"Charm is deceptive, and beauty is fleeting; but a woman who fears the LORD is to be praised."—Proverbs 31:30

When you first met your wife, was she all dolled up? Was this one of the reasons you were attracted to her? What other things about your wife appealed to you then? Make a list; actually write them down, because you will want to refer to these as you work through your feelings about her current personal appearance.

It is natural for you to delight in your companion looking her best. There is pleasure, satisfaction, and perhaps a bit of pride in having an attractive woman at your side. Now as you look at your bride you see a different person, at least physically, than the one you married. You don't love her any less, but something is different inside you when you see her without makeup, her hair disheveled, and perhaps a few pounds heavier. If you are honest, can you identify disappointment, disapproval, or exasperation within yourself? Or maybe helplessness because you can't get her to care enough to make changes?

The changes must come from you. That list you made . . . one by one, draw from it and tell your beloved what you love so much about her. The more you focus on these attributes, the better she will feel about herself, and the less you will concentrate on her physical state.

How will you praise your wife today?

Week 14 Reflections

Day 1: This week's verse in full, or a portion thereof:

____

____

____

Day 2: This verse empowers me to:

____

____

____

Day 3: My response to the entreaty at the end of the message:

____

____

____

Day 4: What I most appreciate about my wife this day/week:

____

____

____

Day 5: Prayer:

____

____

____

Week 15   When your wife rebuffs your sexual advances . . .

"Be joyful in hope, patient in affliction, faithful in prayer."
—Romans 12:13

Frustration, not only physically and emotionally, leaves you feeling helpless and beyond exasperated. You have tried everything from flowers to a romantic evening, and still your wife not only doesn't show interest in making love to you, but blatantly refuses your attention.

Is it possible your wife suffers from a physical condition that causes her pain during intimacy? Or do you believe she is withholding sex for another reason? For example, is there something from her past—or your past—that is a contributing factor? Regardless, it is vital to get to the root of the problem.

Praying together—for each other and for yourselves—for wisdom, mercy, and grace is the first step. Praying to love each other unconditionally, regardless of the circumstances, is also a life-giving step. Close behind is trusting God to work with each of you in His time as you keep your eyes on Him, not on the situation before you. And as important as all these, is sharing spiritual intimacy by studying the Bible together in your home.

Healing takes time and patience. And sometimes requires couples counseling.

God encourages you to be joyful in hope. Patient in affliction. And faithful in prayer.

Will you allow the joy of God's presence fill you with hope for intimacy with your wife?

Week 15 Reflections

Day 1: This week's verse in full, or a portion thereof:

____

____

____

Day 2: This verse empowers me to:

____

____

____

Day 3: My response to the entreaty at the end of the message:

____

____

____

Day 4: What I most appreciate about my wife this day/week:

____

____

____

Day 5: Prayer:

____

____

____

55

Week 16   When your wife disregards your need to be left alone for private time . . .

"He reached down from on high and took hold of me; he drew me out of deep waters."—Psalms 18:16

When you need your space, simply put, you need your space. Most likely it isn't about getting away from your spouse but rather retreating to refuel, to reenergize. To physically, mentally, and spiritually recuperate or refocus.

If your wife isn't one who needs alone time and gets her energy from being around others, then she doesn't have a frame of reference for how you replenish your empty emotional and spiritual bucket.

The Myers-Briggs Personality Inventory is available for free online through several websites. By taking this test, you may gain insight about yourself and your loved one. While this assessment is not infallible—although it has been proven to be valid and reliable—it is a starting place to better understand yourself and your wife. This instrument, and others like it, can reveal your strengths, weaknesses, and blind-spots.

Perhaps the best outcome of both of you taking this test is that you will reach an appreciation for your differences. With this advantage, you can move forward to make changes, to come to agreements, to honor each other's needs.

Will you take the time to follow through with a personality test, knowing there are no right or wrong answers or results, but rather useful information and insights?

Week 16 Reflections

Day 1: This week's verse in full, or a portion thereof:

____

____

____

Day 2: This verse empowers me to:

____

____

____

Day 3: My response to the entreaty at the end of the message:

____

____

____

Day 4: What I most appreciate about my wife this day/week:

____

____

____

Day 5: Prayer:

____

____

____

Week 17   When your wife has her friends over much of the time . . .

"Come to me, all you who are weary and burdened, and I will give you rest."—Matthew 11:28

If you relish coming home from work to a quiet house but are apprehensive about walking through the door for fear it is filled with your wife's friends, do you find your muscles tightening or your jaw clenching? If this is a pattern, do you dread the way the rest of the evening may go?

Did the Myers-Briggs test confirm your need for alone time to reenergize? Did it corroborate your wife's need to be around people? If yes to both of these questions, it is essential for discussion regarding how you can each get your needs met without depriving one or the other of you.

For example, could you suggest to your wife that she has her friends over at another time when you won't be home? Or ask her to meet them someplace else? Or, maybe this is a time when you go to the garage to tinker, or take a jog around the neighborhood, or sit outside cooling your heels with a glass of iced tea?

Whatever solution you agree upon, it is important to champion each other for coming up with something workable. And to validate each other's modus operandi.

How can you apply Matthew 11:28 to the times when you are weary and need rest?

Week 17 Reflections

Day 1: This week's verse in full, or a portion thereof:

____

____

____

Day 2: This verse empowers me to:

____

____

____

Day 3: My response to the entreaty at the end of the message:

____

____

____

Day 4: What I most appreciate about my wife this day/week:

____

____

____

Day 5: Prayer:

____

____

____

Week 18   When your wife complains about you to her friends . . .

"'no weapon forged against you will prevail, and you will refute every tongue that accuses you. This is the heritage of the servants of the LORD, *and this is their vindication from me,' declares the* LORD.*"*—Isaiah 54:17

Well, if your wife's complaints aren't a kick in the shins. Especially when it seems you have been getting along so well. And especially since what your wife is nitpicking about has no merit. At least as far as you can tell.

How can your wife be so far off base? But wait. Have you missed seeing the truth of her grievances? Or is the reality somewhere in between?

The good news is, God promises to refute that which is not true. This is your heritage. This is your vindication.

So, how do you arrive at this?

Of course, the first step is to come before the Lord in humility, and in a deep love for your wife. Because then defensiveness and revenge have no room to set up shop, either in your head or in your home. Once your intentions are pure, now it is time to admit to your wife what you overheard, and that you are surprised at what she said.

When you do this in gentleness and sincerity, leave it up to God to convict her and to encourage her to be open and honest with you. 63

Can you forgive the woman you love for her words? What will it take to move past this?

Week 18 Reflections

Day 1: This week's verse in full, or a portion thereof:

____

____

____

Day 2: This verse empowers me to:

____

____

____

Day 3: My response to the entreaty at the end of the message:

____

____

____

Day 4: What I most appreciate about my wife this day/week:

____

____

____

Day 5: Prayer:

____

____

____

65

Week 19   When your wife nags you to do things . . .

"For if you possess these qualities [faith, goodness, knowledge, self-control, perseverance, godliness, mutual affection, love] in increasing measure, they will keep you from being ineffective and unproductive in your knowledge of our Lord Jesus Christ."—2 Peter 1:8

There is this thought: "You will get it done. You don't need your wife to remind you every six months." And this: "When your wife asks you to do something you better be putting your shoes on before she's done asking."

It's good to laugh about every day dive-bombing swallows—those pesky pests that never seem to go away. Humor can help you tackle even the most humdrum and annoying tasks. For there is no honor in being ineffective and unproductive in your faith or in your home.

The above verse tells how to avoid being unfruitful: Have faith, goodness, knowledge, self-control, perseverance, godliness, mutual affection, and love in increasing measure.

As you grow in faith you will want to do things for your loved one. You will want to be good to her and do things for her just as Christ is and does for you. This knowledge of Jesus helps you with perspective and desire, and will enhance your self-control, perseverance, and godliness. As you show affection and love to your wife, watch your relationship be strengthened and grow deeper emotionally, physically, and spiritually.

What will you do today that you have been putting off? How can you find the humor in it and go about it joyfully?

67

Week 19 Reflections

Day 1: This week's verse in full, or a portion thereof:

____

____

____

Day 2: This verse empowers me to:

____

____

____

Day 3: My response to the entreaty at the end of the message:

____

____

____

Day 4: What I most appreciate about my wife this day/week:

____

____

____

Day 5: Prayer:

____

____

____

Week 20   When your wife insists you accompany her to events you can't stand . . .

"Be devoted to one another in love. Honor one another above yourselves."—Romans 12:10

What are these occasions you detest? The opera or musicals? Weddings? Game nights?

What is there about them you dislike? By identifying this, it may help in presenting your case when you discuss this issue with your wife. Or not.

Even if it doesn't get you off the hook, you will have a better understanding of why you don't want to go. Examine yourself to see if this is an act of selfishness or whether the event in question causes an intense internal reaction related to your past experiences. Or perhaps the event means you will be thrown into the midst of a horde of people where you get so uncomfortable that you become stressed beyond your limits. This is helpful information for your wife to know about you.

You know from scripture you can do all things through Christ who strengthens you (Philippians 4:14). You also know from the Bible that God gives you what you need (Philippians 4:19).

That said, what kind of compromise is possible with your wife, especially after you have discussed all aspects of this issue? And especially after you understand why she loves to have you accompany her on these outings.

How can the two of you honor one another above yourselves?

Week 20 Reflections

Day 1: This week's verse in full, or a portion thereof:

Day 2: This verse empowers me to:

Day 3: My response to the entreaty at the end of the message:

Day 4: What I most appreciate about my wife this day/week:

Day 5: Prayer:

Week 21   When your wife is a backseat driver . . .

"Fools show their annoyance at once, but the prudent overlook an insult."—Proverbs 12:16

You've got things under control. You know where you are going and what you are doing. For some reason, your wife doesn't think so, and she lets you know it. Or maybe she doesn't say anything but grabs the dash or stiffens her body, bracing for a collision. Is this an insult to your driving expertise? Does this trigger annoyance in you? If so, how do you respond to this internal reaction?

The Bible calls you a fool if you show annoyance. Scripture calls you wise if you overlook your wife's behavior/words.

So, how do you dodge being called a fool? Not showing annoyance sounds simple. Except that it is easier said than done. Just like it is easier said than done to overlook an insult. Especially in the heat of the moment—in the midst of traffic. Horns blaring, cars weaving, and your wife's voice coming at you as fast as cars whizzing by, all create confusion and stress.

Sounds like a recipe for an emotional eruption. Yet, with the Holy Spirit within you and Jesus as your chauffeur, you can wheel away from your human tendency to speak not-so-nice words to your wife. This takes practice. Take a deep breath. Fill your lungs with air while filling your mind with memorized verses.

With what verses will you arm yourself to draw upon in situations like this?

Week 21 Reflections

Day 1: This week's verse in full, or a portion thereof:

____

____

____

Day 2: This verse empowers me to:

____

____

____

Day 3: My response to the entreaty at the end of the message:

____

____

____

Day 4: What I most appreciate about my wife this day/week:

____

____

____

Day 5: Prayer:

____

____

____

Week 22   When your wife insists on always being right . . .

"Be perfect, therefore, as your heavenly Father is perfect."—
Matthew 5:48

The Greek word *teleios*—perfect—means completeness or maturity. God calls you to this standard, providing . . .

Tools for Your Growth:

- The Bible:
    - "Your statutes are my delight; they are my counselors."—Psalm 119:24
    - "I will run the way of Your commandments [with purpose], For You will give me a heart that is willing."—Psalms 119:32 (AMP)
- Prayer: "Hear my prayer, O LORD, and give ear to my cry; hold not your peace at my tears!—Psalm 39:12 (ESV)
- Sermons: "For the preaching of the cross is to them that perish foolishness; but unto us which are saved it is the power of God."—1 Corinthians 1:18 (KJV)
- Men's Study Groups: "And let us consider how we may spur one another on toward love and good deeds, not giving up meeting together . . . but encouraging one another"—Hebrews 10:24-25
- Christian Music: ""Let the message of Christ dwell among you richly as you teach and admonish one another with all

wisdom through psalms, hymns, and songs from the Spirit, singing to God with gratitude in your hearts."—Colossians 3:16

So, even though your wife insists on being right, the response God requires of you in these situations is for you to be mature in your response to her.

How will you build into your daily routine the tools above to help you be mature in responding to your wife, regardless the situation?

Week 22 Reflections

Day 1: This week's verse in full, or a portion thereof:

____

____

____

Day 2: This verse empowers me to:

____

____

____

Day 3: My response to the entreaty at the end of the message:

____

____

____

Day 4: What I most appreciate about my wife this day/week:

____

____

____

Day 5: Prayer:

____

____

____

Week 23   When your wife consistently causes you to be late for gatherings . . .

"Starting a quarrel is like breaching a dam, so drop the matter before a dispute breaks out."—Proverbs 17:14

If your wife isn't ready to go when you are, how do you handle it, especially when you know you'll be late? And particularly if promptness is high on your list of values.

Most likely lateness isn't a trait your wife suddenly manifested. If this is the case, how did you deal with it when you started dating? Were you more patient and accepting then because you were infatuated and wanted to woo her into your heart?

She is still that woman. If you now get irritated, it is you who has changed. Simply stated, if you changed this way, then with a little understanding and a bit of effort, you can change back. It beats starting a quarrel. No one wins when the dam is breached, flooding your home with torrents of angry or accusing words.

Discussing this issue before the situation yet again arises, when you are both calm and congenial, hopefully will lead to a workable solution. Such as, going in separate cars, or whatever you both can agree upon.

Or, you can work on being patient and changing your attitude to: *In the grand scheme of things being late is not the end of the world. I don't want to lose someone I love to gain something so inconsequential.*

What solution you are willing to work on and can live with?

Week 23 Reflections

Day 1: This week's verse in full, or a portion thereof:

____

____

____

Day 2: This verse empowers me to:

____

____

____

Day 3: My response to the entreaty at the end of the message:

____

____

____

Day 4: What I most appreciate about my wife this day/week:

____

____

____

Day 5: Prayer:

____

____

Week 24   When your wife micromanages you . . .

"The one who has knowledge uses words with restraint, and whoever has understanding is even-tempered."—Proverbs 17:27

When your wife tells you what to do, understandably, you get exasperated, or possibly have a stronger reaction. You want to be the head of the household as God has intended. Not necessarily because you demand control, but because you want to utilize the skills and knowledge with which the Lord has blessed you.

It is frustrating when your attempts to lead are questioned or thwarted.

When you married your loved one, did you admire her independent nature and strong will, and that she was stalwart in her opinions? If so, these are still character traits you can respect in her.

Applying Proverbs 17:27, this knowledge and understanding of your wife empowers you to use words with restraint and be even-tempered. It does not, however, imply you are to relinquish the leadership role in your household.

That said, would you want your wife to relinquish her nature when it is what emboldens her to be a woman of God?

If you have taken the Myers-Briggs Inventory, having gained a greater understanding of who each of you are, prayerful consideration and conversation around this issue of "micromanagement" can lead to a better balance of management in your marriage.

How does knowledge of who you are in Christ and knowledge of the Word of God encourage you to embrace your role—and your wife—in this situation?

Week 24 Reflections

Day 1: This week's verse in full, or a portion thereof:

____

____

____

Day 2: This verse empowers me to:

____

____

____

Day 3: My response to the entreaty at the end of the message:

____

____

____

Day 4: What I most appreciate about my wife this day/week:

____

____

____

Day 5: Prayer:

____

____

____

85

Week 25   When your wife doesn't respect your decisions . . .

"Then I will ever sing in praise of your name and fulfill my vows day after day."—Psalm 61:8

When you wife doesn't respect your decisions, this is in direct correlation to Week 24's issue—when your spouse micromanages you. Last week's verse encouraged you to be even-tempered and use your words with restraint. This week, God's Word aims to inspire you, to nurture your faith and the vows you took at the marriage altar.

In the midst of being disrespected, you may find it challenging to praise God and fulfill your vows. Not just this moment, but day after day. That is a tall order. Especially if you are running low on emotional and energy reserves. Disrespect chips away at self-esteem, your love for your wife, and your desire to keep on keeping on.

Which is precisely what the enemy intends.

God has armed you with spiritual weapons to withstand Satan's attacks. Buckle up the belt of truth—(your struggle is not against your wife but against evil forces); put on the breastplate of righteousness—(sing praises to God); fit your feet with readiness to peace—(fulfill your vows); take up the shield of faith—(put out the flaming arrows of the devil); take the helmet of salvation, and grasp the sword of the Spirit—

(God's Word is defensive as it protects, and acts in the offensive for counterattack).

How can knowing your battle is not against your wife but against Satan empower you to sing praises and fulfill your vows?

Week 25 Reflections

Day 1: This week's verse in full, or a portion thereof:

____

____

____

Day 2: This verse empowers me to:

____

____

____

Day 3: My response to the entreaty at the end of the message:

____

____

____

Day 4: What I most appreciate about my wife this day/week:

____

____

____

Day 5: Prayer:

____

____

____

89

Week 26   When your wife isn't appreciative of things you do . . .

"Now may the Lord of peace himself give you peace at all times in every way. The Lord be with all of you."
—2 Thessalonians 3:16

Is it really possible for you to have peace when you try your hardest to please your wife and your efforts go unappreciated? According the above verse, yes. And not only in this situation but at all times in every way.

How is this possible?

God is with you in this and all circumstances, and when you turn your eyes away from what is going on around you to focus on Him, as the song, "Turn Your Eyes Upon Jesus" says, "the things of the earth grow strangely dim in the light of His glory and grace."

As you sing or listen to this song and quiet your heart and spirit, drawing near to Jesus, imagine how He sees you. If your efforts to do things around the house and for your wife are sincere, how much must Christ appreciate your labor!

At this point it is easier to embrace Colossians 3:23-24: "Whatever you do, work at it with all your heart, as working for the Lord, not for human masters, since you know that you will receive an inheritance from the Lord as a reward. It is the Lord Christ you are serving."

An inheritance from the Lord as a reward. Wow!

Knowing you are serving Jesus, how does this make doing things for your wife easier?

Week 26 Reflections

Day 1: This week's verse in full, or a portion thereof:

____

____

____

Day 2: This verse empowers me to:

____

____

____

Day 3: My response to the entreaty at the end of the message:

____

____

____

Day 4: What I most appreciate about my wife this day/week:

____

____

____

Day 5: Prayer:

____

____

____

Week 27   When your wife keeps a laundry list of everything you've done wrong . . .

"'I, even I, am he who blots out your transgressions, for my own sake, and remembers your sins no more. Review the past for me, let us argue the matter together; state the case for your innocence.'"—Isaiah 43:25-26

You have been forgiven . . . by the Lord. However, when your wife hasn't moved on from your transgressions, it is difficult to step forward in your marriage relationship with a clean slate. The stains of your past seem to taint whatever you do now.

Where do you go from here? Work harder at pleasing your wife? Quit trying to do things right? Ignore her fault-finding and keep doing whatever seems right anyway? Or do you say to yourself, *"I can find the good in this. My wife has a mind like a steel trap. How can I tap into this characteristic she has and find the silver lining?"*

If you seize this last path and apply Romans 8:28: "And we know that in all things God works for the good of those who love him, who have been called according to his purpose.", you will free yourself from the accusations and trap the devil sets for you when this laundry list is aired. You will be liberated to argue these matters with the Lord, who is your shield and defender.

Can you see the good in this situation? What purpose do you see God using you for in this situation?

Week 27 Reflections

Day 1: This week's verse in full, or a portion thereof:

____

____

____

Day 2: This verse empowers me to:

____

____

____

Day 3: My response to the entreaty at the end of the message:

____

____

____

Day 4: What I most appreciate about my wife this day/week:

____

____

____

Day 5: Prayer:

____

____

____

Week 28 When your wife complains about how much money you earn . . .

"Do not seek revenge or bear a grudge against anyone among your people, but love your neighbor as yourself. I am the LORD."—Leviticus 19:18

Which is harder for you to bear . . . a dripping faucet or your wife complaining about how much you earn? The former is easily fixed. The latter, not so much.

Of course, you could find a better-paying job. That is if you don't get satisfaction from the one you have. But if you enjoy your work and find reward in a job well done, your salary is not nearly as important. To you, anyway. What it comes down to is passion vs. money.

Loving what you do has an impact on your sense of self-worth, which increases your productivity and pride in what you do. This is part of what motivates you to get out of bed in the morning and head out the door to your place of employment. And away from the voice of derision, for once away from this, your stress is reduced and as such your body is healthier.

Still, it is important to ask yourself these questions, and lift them to God:

Do I earn enough to adequately support my family? Could I be just as happy in another job with higher pay but essentially doing the same type of work? Do I need to consider adding a part-time job to my schedule? What would you have me do, Lord?

How can you deal with this issue in a godly way?

Week 28 Reflections

Day 1: This week's verse in full, or a portion thereof:

____

____

____

Day 2: This verse empowers me to:

____

____

____

Day 3: My response to the entreaty at the end of the message:

____

____

____

Day 4: What I most appreciate about my wife this day/week:

____

____

____

Day 5: Prayer:

____

____

____

Week 29   When your wife overspends your household budget . . .

" 'The silver is mine and the gold is mine,' declares LORD *Almighty."*—Haggai 2:8

It is a vulnerable position to be in when your spouse spends beyond your means. Does it seem as if you are spiraling into a bottomless abyss with no way out? Most likely you have already tried to discuss this with your wife, but to no avail. And if you have attempted this conversation more than once, does she accuse you of not understanding her needs, or of badgering her?

Would your wife be open to attending group workshops on budgeting? Many churches hold this type of help for parishioners. Perhaps if your spouse is encouraged by other Christian women, she would be more willing to take this issue seriously. If she is unwilling to do something like this, there are great workbooks on financial planning for peace of mind on the market which might help you proceed, even if on your own.

The reality is, everything you have belongs to the Lord. So, in actuality, your spouse is drawing from the Lord's bank. If you consider the situation in this manner, can you then leave it in God's hands to convict your loved one to be financially responsible?

In addition to prayer, what steps will you take to address this matter?

Week 29 Reflections

Day 1: This week's verse in full, or a portion thereof:

____

____

____

Day 2: This verse empowers me to:

____

____

____

Day 3: My response to the entreaty at the end of the message:

____

____

____

Day 4: What I most appreciate about my wife this day/week:

____

____

____

Day 5: Prayer:

____

____

____

Week 30   When your wife demands to know where you are at all times . . .

"Husbands . . . be considerate as you live with your wives, and treat them with respect as the weaker partner and as heirs with you of the gracious gift of life, so that nothing will hinder your prayers."—1 Peter 3:7

Although your spouse wanting to be aware of your daily routine is normal, if she insists on knowing where you are every minute, most likely this is her trust issue.

If she checks in with you multiple times a day via a phone call or text messaging, how do you handle it? Do you ignore her attempts? If so, does this cause a fight? Do you respond immediately to stay out of the dog house but then get resentful? Or do you wait the right amount of time for *you* to be in control of your time before you return the call or text?

So, what do you do, since you want to show respect to your wife? It is considerate to let her know you are leaving the house, what time you will be home for dinner, how long you will be gone, etc. These all make for a healthy relationship.

Showing respect in these ways while at the same time letting her know her constant contact throughout the day hints at lack of trust, builds unity. Then pray together for God's help in this.

How would God have you go about your day?

Week 30 Reflections

Day 1: This week's verse in full, or a portion thereof:

____

____

____

Day 2: This verse empowers me to:

____

____

____

Day 3: My response to the entreaty at the end of the message:

____

____

____

Day 4: What I most appreciate about my wife this day/week:

____

____

____

Day 5: Prayer:

____

____

____

Week 31   When your wife refuses to socialize with your friends and their wives . . .

"It [love] does not dishonor others, it is not self-seeking, it is not easily angered, it keeps no record of wrongs."
—1 Corinthians 13:5

Socializing with other couples is one way to share fun experiences while meeting with friends in common. When your wife won't accompany you to get-togethers, do you get angry, do you feel awkward showing up alone, do you make excuses for her once you arrive without her? Then as her refusal to join you repeats itself, do you remind her of all the times you've done things with her you didn't want to, then proceed to present her record of wrongs?

All these are very common responses—behaviors that undermine the marriage. What do you believe is the core issue here with your wife? Shyness? Discomfort around people because of something in the past? Your friends are obnoxious? Or do you dishonor her with disparaging comments, embarrassing and shaming her in front of others?

For unity to be a firm foundation in your relationship, these critical components must be identified and discussed. Maybe that means counseling. Perhaps you will come to an understanding on your own.

Regardless, it doesn't mean you must give up meeting with your friends. And it doesn't require your wife to join you. What it is important is that you honor one another's choices.

What other activities can you share that you both love to do?

105

Week 31 Reflections

Day 1: This week's verse in full, or a portion thereof:

____

____

____

Day 2: This verse empowers me to:

____

____

____

Day 3: My response to the entreaty at the end of the message:

____

____

____

Day 4: What I most appreciate about my wife this day/week:

____

____

____

Day 5: Prayer:

____

____

____

Week 32   When your wife's whole world is the children, to the exclusion of you . . .

"Let the morning bring me word of your unfailing love, for I have put my trust in you. Show me the way I should go, for to you I entrust my life."—Psalm 143:8

When you wake in the morning to an empty bed because your wife is tending to the children, do you wistfully recall the childless days when you and your loved one started the day with a snuggle? Do you miss seeing the love for you in her eyes? Do you long for her face to brighten as it used to when she looked at you, or her smile when you walked into the room?

Even though things are different now, you know she still loves you. Yet the passion isn't there. Or the alone-time commitment. You also know your wife takes her job as mother seriously, and for that you admire and love her even more. You just wish you didn't feel shut out.

Do you suppose Jesus feels that way with you sometimes? Might He miss the intimacy He shared with you when you first asked Him into your heart? At what point did this start to diminish?

Would you be open to making a date night with your wife to discuss this, and use it as a segue for how you miss emotional, physical, mental intimacy with her? Hopefully this will help your wife see the situation without feeling criticized.

What do you need to do to schedule an away and alone time with your beloved?

Week 32 Reflections

Day 1: This week's verse in full, or a portion thereof:

____

____

____

Day 2: This verse empowers me to:

____

____

____

Day 3: My response to the entreaty at the end of the message:

____

____

____

Day 4: What I most appreciate about my wife this day/week:

____

____

____

Day 5: Prayer:

____

____

____

Week 33   When your wife leaves you out of parenting your children . . .

"No one has ever seen God; but if we love one another, God lives in us and his love is made complete in us."—1 John 4:12

Yet you have never physically seen God, you know you are His child. You know He loves you, and are privileged to be parented by Him.

How do you know these things? Through His Word. Through the Holy Spirit Who lives in you. And through your knowledge and faith that Jesus gave His life for you.

How can your children know you love them? Through the time you spend with them. Through your words spoken in love. Through the evidence you are providing and protecting them. These are all parts of parenting, components your wife can't ignore.

When she leaves you out of parenting, does that mean she says you are too strict or not strict enough in your disciplining, thus she takes charge of this role? Or is it possible she assumes this task because you are exhausted and stressed when you get home from work?

You might be surprised at the whys and wherefores of this issue. Could she be protecting you from conflict with the children? Is she trying to make your life easier and less burdensome? Preceded by prayer, these are questions worth discussing.

At any rate, consider the ways you do contribute to parenting your children, and capitalize on those.

What more can you do to actively participate in being a father?

Week 33 Reflections

Day 1: This week's verse in full, or a portion thereof:

____

____

____

Day 2: This verse empowers me to:

____

____

____

Day 3: My response to the entreaty at the end of the message:

____

____

____

Day 4: What I most appreciate about my wife this day/week:

____

____

____

Day 5: Prayer:

____

____

____

Week 34   When your wife belittles you in front of your children . . .

"Above all, love each other deeply, because love covers over a multitude of sins."—1 Peter 4:8

When does your wife belittle you? Is it after an argument? Is it when you don't do something "right"? Is it when things aren't going well for her? What do you see in your children's eyes when this happens?

One course of action is to have a conversation about this hurtful situation with your wife out of the hearing of little ears. The discussion must not be accusatory or critical, but one where you reveal the hurt you feel from her words. But if the dialogue doesn't produce the results you desire, you are left with addressing the circumstances in a different way.

How do you go about this? Of vital importance is to not belittle your wife in front of your children. Showing how much you love them and their mother will shield you all from the damage hurtful words can cause. You are the role model God has designed for your young ones.

So, when your wife disparages you, do not react, but respond, choosing your words wisely.

E.g. "Honey, I am sorry you feel that way. What can I do to help?" Or "Although your words are hurtful, I love you more than you know." Or, if she would allow, give her a hug.

Next time, will you pause long enough to allow the Holy Spirit to speak through you?

Week 34 Reflections

Day 1: This week's verse in full, or a portion thereof:

____

____

____

Day 2: This verse empowers me to:

____

____

____

Day 3: My response to the entreaty at the end of the message:

____

____

____

Day 4: What I most appreciate about my wife this day/week:

____

____

____

Day 5: Prayer:

____

____

____

Week 35   When your wife punishes you with silence . . .

"Hope deferred makes the heart sick, but a longing fulfilled is a tree of life."—Proverbs 13:12

A loved one's silence, indeed, makes the heart sick. You are left hoping your wife will get past whatever has triggered her silence, and while you wait it thunders through the household. As Proverbs 13:12 states, when your longing is fulfilled, your life is back on track, as is your marriage and peace within your heart and home.

When your wife dishes out the silent treatment, it can be meant to punish, to let you know you have hurt her, or that she needs time away from you for whatever reason. However, because she isn't speaking, you can't really know why she has withdrawn. Trying to figure out what's going on in her mind is likely to cause even more silence if it seems you are oversimplifying the situation. Does this sound familiar?

What to do? There are a couple of ways you can communicate your desire to talk with her. One is simply stating, "I need you to help me understand what your silence is about." Once said, don't push for a response. A second approach is to leave her a note with a similar message. Ask God to lead you to other paths to take.

When your wife does open up, listen. Above all, avoid being defensive. This is an opportunity to hear your wife—to draw close to her.

Ask God to reveal if there is anything in your behavior that triggers silence in your wife.

Week 35 Reflections

Day 1: This week's verse in full, or a portion thereof:

____

____

____

Day 2: This verse empowers me to:

____

____

____

Day 3: My response to the entreaty at the end of the message:

____

____

____

Day 4: What I most appreciate about my wife this day/week:

____

____

____

Day 5: Prayer:

____

____

____

Week 36   When your wife constantly interrupts you . . .

"Be completely humble and gentle; be patient, bearing with one another in love. Make every effort to keep the unity of the Spirit through the bond of peace."—Ephesians 4:2-3

When your wife interrupts you, do you feel unheard or dismissed? Whatever you experience when this happens, it is difficult, to say the least, to be completely humble, gentle, patient and bearing with your wife in love. Beyond those biblical encouragements, God expects you to make every effort to keep the unity of the Spirit through the bond of peace.

Whew! Well, Jesus never promised God doesn't expect much from you. But He did promise that His Holy Spirit inside you would give you words to speak: "for the Holy Spirit will teach you at that time what you should say."—Luke 12:12

Granted, Jesus spoke this in the context of when you are standing before rulers and authorities, but still, if the Holy Spirit can help you not to worry about what to say in this situation, why wouldn't He offer the same in your marriage relationship?

Silently ask God to help your wife realize she interrupts you. Before you begin talking, ask your wife to allow you to finish what you want to say. Let her know her input is important, and so is what you contribute to the conversation.

If she continues to interrupt, pause and silently ask the Holy Spirit how to respond.

Will you grant the Holy Spirit permission to speak through you in this situation?

123

Week 36 Reflections

Day 1: This week's verse in full, or a portion thereof:

____

____

____

Day 2: This verse empowers me to:

____

____

____

Day 3: My response to the entreaty at the end of the message:

____

____

____

Day 4: What I most appreciate about my wife this day/week:

____

____

____

Day 5: Prayer:

____

____

____

125

Week 37   When your wife is gone much of the time . . .

"You, LORD, are my lamp; the LORD turns my darkness into light."—2 Samuel 22:29

Coming home from work to enter a dark house is a cold and unwelcoming experience. The same goes for when you look forward to spending the evening with your wife only to be told she is going to her book club or one of her activities.

Alone time is great some of the time, but when it becomes the norm, a dark cloud shrouds your relationship. Does it seem the light has gone out of your marriage and you find yourself in spiritual darkness as a result?

This is where the enemy wants to take you. God, however, desires to turn your darkness into light. When you are in His presence, there is no room for darkness. If you end up alone and that cloud of doom descends upon you, call on the Lord to lift you up out of the pit and into His company. Spend time in the Bible. Put on Christian music. Reach out to your friends for prayer. Submit to God, rebuke the devil and he will flee from you.

Certainly, you can let your wife know how much you enjoy being around her. How much it means to you to have her by your side, but if this doesn't encourage her to spend more time at home, you still have the Lord who will never leave you. Soak up His light and presence.

How does God's presence lift you out of darkness?

Week 37 Reflections

Day 1: This week's verse in full, or a portion thereof:

____

____

____

Day 2: This verse empowers me to:

____

____

____

Day 3: My response to the entreaty at the end of the message:

____

____

____

Day 4: What I most appreciate about my wife this day/week:

____

____

____

Day 5: Prayer:

____

____

____

Week 38   When your wife constantly wants to know what you are thinking . . .

"You have captivated my heart, my sister, my bride; you have captivated my heart with one glance of your eyes, with one jewel of your necklace."—Song of Solomon 4:9

Playfulness can come into play when you want to dodge revealing your private thoughts to your wife. When she asks what you are thinking, creative responses are a marvelous ally.

Taking a page from the Song of Solomon is a place to start. How about quoting the verse above with a twinkle in your eye and a smile on your lips? Or drawing from Elizabeth Barrett Browning when she penned Sonnet 43 during the courtship of Robert Browning: "How do I love thee? Let me count the ways."?

However, you may not be into quotes and want to come up with your own words, e.g. "I'm thinking of your beauty." "I'm thinking about how I love you more than the day we married." "What's running through my mind right at this moment are all the things I appreciate about you." (Then list them off.)

Instead of getting irritated at your wife's questions, you can involve her in the fun of this. Filling up your response bucket ahead of time will help you from being caught unaware and unprepared.

Can Romans 13:8 fit in this situation?—"Owe no one anything, [i.e. your thoughts], except to love each other, for the one who loves another has fulfilled the law."

Right now what playful responses come to mind?

Week 38 Reflections

Day 1: This week's verse in full, or a portion thereof:

____

____

____

Day 2: This verse empowers me to:

____

____

____

Day 3: My response to the entreaty at the end of the message:

____

____

____

Day 4: What I most appreciate about my wife this day/week:

____

____

____

Day 5: Prayer:

____

____

____

Week 39   When your wife doesn't trust you and goes through your things . . .

"Though one may be overpowered, two can defend themselves. A cord of three strands is not quickly broken."
—Ecclesiastes 4:12

When you took your wedding vows, God joined you and your bride together as one. And as one, you traverse through life as a team, able to defend yourselves from hardships, tragedies, and attacks from the enemy. But this defense is only as strong as humanly possible. Especially when the devil butts in to cause mistrust and divisiveness. At this point Satan nudges your wife toward seeing you as her enemy and you to regard her as your adversary when she rifles through your things. Satan is an accuser and a liar, whispering untruths in the ears of believers.

When God joined you and your loved one together in Holy matrimony, He purposed for you to reign collectively in the power of the Holy Spirit to defeat assaults from the real enemy. In essence the two of you became one with another—and one with God.

Because God is the third strand in the cord of your relationship, your bonds will not be quickly broken. Hallelujah!

But back to the issue of mistrust . . . is there an unresolved or past issue that bears credence to your wife's mistrust? Whether in her past, your past, or recently in your relationship? If so and left unaddressed, this leaves the enemy with ammunition.

What action is the Holy Spirit encouraging you to take in this situation?

Week 39 Reflections

Day 1: This week's verse in full, or a portion thereof:

____

____

____

Day 2: This verse empowers me to:

____

____

____

Day 3: My response to the entreaty at the end of the message:

____

____

____

Day 4: What I most appreciate about my wife this day/week:

____

____

____

Day 5: Prayer:

____

____

____

133

Week 40   When your wife falsely accuses you of having an affair . . .

" . . . But while Joseph was there in the prison, the LORD was with him; he showed him kindness and granted him favor in the eyes of the prison warden. . . . the LORD was with Joseph and gave him success in whatever he did."—Genesis 39:20, 21, 23

Joseph was a man of God dedicated to doing right. However, that didn't protect him from false accusations. Nor does your commitment to the Lord and to your wife shield you from untrue allegations.

How did Joseph handle this incriminating situation? The Bible doesn't say if Joseph tried to defend himself, but rather that he escaped from the clutches of Potiphar's wife and went about his honorable business. Although he had circumvented committing adultery, he didn't evade a prison sentence. One might think God had abandoned him. Yet the opposite was true. Even while imprisoned, the Lord was faithful, showing him kindness and giving Joseph success in all he did.

The Lord's faithfulness is equally committed to you. He is your defender, just as He was Joseph's. Joseph depended on God alone. He had no doubt God defended and protected him. As such, even when incarcerated Joseph knew he was not forsaken, and that his salvation and honor depended upon God.

Acting in Christlikeness, saying nothing to untrue accusations, and leaving it in God's hands will garner you justice—whether now or eventually.

Even though it may be hard to not defend yourself, will you trust God with your honor?

Week 40 Reflections

Day 1: This week's verse in full, or a portion thereof:

____

____

____

Day 2: This verse empowers me to:

____

____

____

Day 3: My response to the entreaty at the end of the message:

____

____

____

Day 4: What I most appreciate about my wife this day/week:

____

____

____

Day 5: Prayer:

____

____

____

Week 41   When your wife flirts with other men . . .

"So husbands ought to love their own wives as their own bodies;
he who loves his wife loves himself."—Ephesians 5:28

Keeping this verse as a foundation and guiding beacon fortifies you to demonstrate your level of commitment and investment in your marriage.

When you see your wife flirting with other men, do you doubt her love for you? If your answer is, "No, I know she loves me." then the next question is, does her flirting trigger jealousy within you? If this answer is "yes" then perhaps your insecurity is worthy of examination. Have you told your wife her flirting bothers you? If you haven't expressed your feelings, what keeps you from doing so? Do you fear your wife's flirtation is an attempt for attention or something you aren't giving her?

The bottom line is, flirting is an outward indication of inner needs not being met—in both of you. To ignore this by laughing off this behavior as "It's just done in fun." or "It doesn't go any further than that." Or "It doesn't hurt anything." is a lie from the enemy and an opportunity for the devil to divide and conquer.

There are lots of questions to consider around this issue. Ones that necessitate immediate and careful attention which may be best pursued with a counselor or pastor.

How can your message to your wife help you work through this issue?

Week 41 Reflections

Day 1: This week's verse in full, or a portion thereof:

____

____

____

Day 2: This verse empowers me to:

____

____

____

Day 3: My response to the entreaty at the end of the message:

____

____

____

Day 4: What I most appreciate about my wife this day/week:

____

____

____

Day 5: Prayer:

____

____

____

Week 42   When your wife compares you to other men . . .

"Hatred stirs up conflict, but love covers over all wrongs."
—Proverbs 10:12

Being compared to other men by your wife is tough to take. Especially if her words ring true. You are aware of your own shortcomings and don't need to be reminded of them. On the other hand, if your wife touts someone else's virtues or strengths, it doesn't mean you have to take this personally. Still, if she out and out states more than asks, "Why can't you be more like so and so?" . . . this is a different matter and not one which requires an answer. Rather, this kind of comparison is generally meant as a criticism and one certain to ignite conflict, or at least is intended to chip away at your self-esteem.

There are many different responses you can give when these comparisons come. The first and most common is a tit for tat by immediately comparing your wife to one of her friends. Biblically speaking, this is a hateful, spiteful reaction sure to stir up conflict.

The better way to go? Love your wife. Respond in love, for love indeed covers over all wrongs—yours and hers.

What would responding in love look like to you? Scripture is jam-packed with helpful verses—all of which promise to lead you to the healthiest relationship you can have with the one you love.

Make a list of verses to help you when your wife compares you to others.

Week 42 Reflections

Day 1: This week's verse in full, or a portion thereof:

____

____

____

Day 2: This verse empowers me to:

____

____

____

Day 3: My response to the entreaty at the end of the message:

____

____

____

Day 4: What I most appreciate about my wife this day/week:

____

____

____

Day 5: Prayer:

____

____

____

Week 43   When your wife hides things from you . . .

"Be kind and compassionate to one another, forgiving each other, just as in Christ God forgave you."—Ephesians 4:32

When you discover your wife is hiding something from you, it is important to understand why. E.g. she may be afraid what she is hiding might hurt you. Or your bride might not feel safe sharing things with you.

Further, how did you discover she is hiding something? Had her behavior changed and you became suspicious? Did you go looking for evidence? If you did, did you disregard her privacy? And now that you know, how will you confront her in a godly manner without her feeling violated or accused?

Simply said, mutual trust has been broken. It is up to you to create a safe environment to discuss, not confront, what is going on. It may take time for your wife to open up. Insisting she talk will only increase the non-safety matter. And, she may never tell you the truth. Still, make yourself available to your wife to discuss things, to be emotionally intimate with her.

Treat this as the perfect opportunity to be kind and compassionate to your wife, to forgive her. God has forgiven you more than seventy times seven, so is it too much to ask you to do the same for the one you love?

How can knowing you have hidden things from your wife help you forgive her?

Week 43 Reflections

Day 1: This week's verse in full, or a portion thereof:

____

____

____

Day 2: This verse empowers me to:

____

____

____

Day 3: My response to the entreaty at the end of the message:

____

____

____

Day 4: What I most appreciate about my wife this day/week:

____

____

____

Day 5: Prayer:

____

____

____

Week 44   When your wife abuses alcohol/drugs . . .

"It [love] always protects, always trusts, always hopes, always perseveres."—1 Corinthians 13:7

Your wife's abuse of alcohol or drugs not only affects her physical, emotional, mental, and spiritual health, but yours as well. Important for you to know is that monitoring her use of substances, throwing away bottles or vials, pleading with her to stop, covering for her behaviors, etc. are not only unproductive, but unhealthy for you to do.

If you don't know where to turn, pick up the phone and call for help. Many great resources are available, one of which is Al-Anon. In this support group you gain coping skills for yourself while learning what your spouse is experiencing. Taking care of yourself before attempting an intervention is vital. Then you will be better equipped to be supportive.

Once you feel ready to talk with your loved one, research ways to speak with her and make a plan for your conversation. Choose a time when she is sober, be direct yet gentle and loving, acknowledge the challenges she is struggling with, ask her what she would like to do to get her life under control, avoid giving her an ultimatum, and know in advance treatment options. Focus on results—e.g. better health, fewer missed work days, etc. Most likely, your wife will be in denial, so be patient and pray. Rebuke the enemy's hold on her. Trust God with her life.

What steps will you take to trust, hope, and persevere in this matter?

Week 44 Reflections

Day 1: This week's verse in full, or a portion thereof:

____

____

____

Day 2: This verse empowers me to:

____

____

____

Day 3: My response to the entreaty at the end of the message:

____

____

____

Day 4: What I most appreciate about my wife this day/week:

____

____

____

Day 5: Prayer:

____

____

____

147

Week 45   When your wife is self-absorbed/selfish . . .

"Do nothing out of selfish ambition or vain conceit. Rather, in humility value others above yourselves, not looking to your own interests but each of you to the interests of the others."
—Philippians 2:3-4

When your wife behaves in self-absorbed, selfish ways, it is human nature to "give her a taste of her own medicine." It is also tempting to read Philippians 2:3-4 and ask the Lord, "You want me to do nothing out of selfish ambition and not look to my own interests but rather to my wife's, but why should I be the one to follow this verse and not her?" Don't be surprised if God doesn't answer this complaint in the way you want.

Rather, His response will likely be along the lines of what He told Peter in John 21:21, when Jesus told Peter to follow Him. Peter saw the disciple Jesus loved following them, then asked, "Lord, what about him?" Jesus pretty much told Peter it wasn't any of his business and said, "I'm telling *you* to follow me."

That said, you will only grow more resentful if you don't tell your wife you would love to have her help. Thank her when she does an unselfish act. Be on the lookout for these times as it is possible you—in your own self-absorption—haven't noticed them.

Additionally, reconsider what you might see as selfishness, i.e. when your wife spends time with her friends. Women need this camaraderie.

How will memorizing Philippians 2:3-4 help you stay on track for loving your wife?

Week 45 Reflections

Day 1: This week's verse in full, or a portion thereof:

____

____

____

Day 2: This verse empowers me to:

____

____

____

Day 3: My response to the entreaty at the end of the message:

____

____

____

Day 4: What I most appreciate about my wife this day/week:

____

____

____

Day 5: Prayer:

____

____

____

Week 46   When your wife spreads false rumors about you throughout the church . . .

". . . 'Do not fear, for I have redeemed you; I have summoned you by name; you are mine. When you pass through the waters, I will be with you; and when you pass through the rivers, they will not sweep over you. When you walk through the fire, you will not be burned; the flames will not set you ablaze."—Isaiah 43:1-2

Unfortunately, a spouse spreading false rumors—throughout the church no less—is not unheard of. When this happens to you, your brothers and sisters in Christ look at you differently, or if not that, at least they don't know what to think or who to believe. Even if others don't eye you suspiciously, you may think they are doing so. Which affects not only your personal relationships but those within the church community as a whole. The devil seizes this opportunity to tempt parishioners to choose sides in an attempt to divide and conquer. In this way he gets a twofer . . . destroying your marriage and damaging the body of believers.

To dodge that bullet, claim Isaiah 43:1-2. In short, God's got your back, your present, and your future. People falsely accused Jesus, too, so He knows what you are going through. Draw close to Him. Look full in His wonderful face. To repeat the song from Week 26, *the things of this world will grow strangely dim in the light of His glory and grace.* Call up once again "Turn Your Eyes Upon Jesus." Add this to your cell phone's music library.

Will you let the Lord be your defender?

Week 46 Reflections

Day 1: This week's verse in full, or a portion thereof:

____

____

____

Day 2: This verse empowers me to:

____

____

____

Day 3: My response to the entreaty at the end of the message:

____

____

____

Day 4: What I most appreciate about my wife this day/week:

____

____

____

Day 5: Prayer:

____

____

____

Week 47   When your wife lies to you . . .

"I call on the LORD *in my distress, and he answers me. Save me,* LORD, *from lying lips and from deceitful tongues."*
—Psalms 120:1-2

Broken promises and lies are the foundation for mistrust. Trust is one of the most vital components of a marriage. When that is violated, a breakdown of communication follows, even if your wife lies not to hurt you or leave you out of something, but to get herself out of a sticky situation of which you may not be a part.

Regardless, it is important to gently state the truth about the matter and let your wife know you know and that you still love her. If this is a pattern of hers, it is even more vital to bring the lie into the light, for if she believes she is getting away with telling lies, it reinforces the behavior.

Following that, your next step is to forgive—for a couple of reasons. First because God calls us to do so and your relationship with Him is paramount—to grow in your faith and to build your marriage on His statutes. Secondly, forgiving will release you from storing up resentment or anger.

Subsequently, devote yourself to rebuilding trust with your wife. Show her how much you love her and want truth to reign in your home. This may take lots of time and lots of prayer but is worth the investment.

As often as is necessary, repeat Psalms 120:2—"Save me, LORD, **from lying lips and from deceitful tongues."**

Week 47 Reflections

Day 1: This week's verse in full, or a portion thereof:

____

____

____

Day 2: This verse empowers me to:

____

____

____

Day 3: My response to the entreaty at the end of the message:

____

____

____

Day 4: What I most appreciate about my wife this day/week:

____

____

____

Day 5: Prayer:

____

____

____

Week 48   When your wife has an affair . . .

"I have chosen the way of faithfulness; I have set my heart on your laws. I hold fast to your statutes, LORD; do not let me be put to shame."—Psalms 119:30-31

Because you have been faithful and walk firmly in God's statutes, you are in disbelief when your wife cheats on you. You wonder where things went wrong in your relationship, thinking back to how you could have missed signs of things going south between you and the woman you love and committed to for life. Heartbroken, you wonder if there is anything you could have done differently, or if now there is anything you can do to win your wife's love once again.

But then, emotions whirlwind through you. Anger, hatred, humiliation, anxiety, and more invade your thoughts, leaving you confused, depressed, and/or unable to sleep. And leaving you wondering whether or not you want to salvage the marriage . . . if you can ever trust her again.

One of the most important steps you can take is to reach out for help to a man of God trained to walk you through this difficult time. If your wife agrees to marriage counseling, be encouraged. Even at that, going to individual therapy for yourself will give *you* the opportunity to do what you need to in order to heal and move forward in the path God has for you. Be patient with your wife. Be patient with yourself.

What do you sense the Lord leading you to do today?

Week 48 Reflections

Day 1: This week's verse in full, or a portion thereof:

____

____

____

Day 2: This verse empowers me to:

____

____

____

Day 3: My response to the entreaty at the end of the message:

____

____

____

Day 4: What I most appreciate about my wife this day/week:

____

____

____

Day 5: Prayer:

____

____

____

Week 49   When your wife refuses to go with you to marriage counseling . . .

"Mercy, peace and love be yours in abundance."—Jude 1:2

When your wife refuses to accompany you to marriage counseling, your situation may seem hopeless. While restoring the relationship with your wife may seem hopeless, your relationship with Jesus is not. He promises to be with you, providing an abundance of mercy, peace and love to help you through this difficult time. Through Him you can continue to love your wife, allowing the mercy of God flow through you to her. The Lord will help you not give up hope.

Granting mercy to your wife in her decision against counseling means avoiding giving her an ultimatum. Accepting that you can't make your wife do anything will help you let go of trying in vain to change her mind. Attending counseling by yourself will give you tools for becoming the best person you can be, which may change how you interact with your wife.

With individual therapy, even as you grow healthier and stronger and your wife draws further away, you might come to the conclusion that it would be easier to quit trying to make things work with your wife. In fact, that might be the encouragement you receive from your friends. However, the Holy Spirit is your greatest ally. Listen to His voice and leading, for then truly will mercy, peace and love be yours in abundance. Regardless of the outcome.

How is the Holy Spirit encouraging you to stay strong and faithful?

Week 49 Reflections

Day 1: This week's verse in full, or a portion thereof:

____

____

____

Day 2: This verse empowers me to:

____

____

____

Day 3: My response to the entreaty at the end of the message:

____

____

____

Day 4: What I most appreciate about my wife this day/week:

____

____

____

Day 5: Prayer:

____

____

____

Week 50   When your wife asks for a divorce . . .

"My soul is weary with sorrow; strengthen me according to your word."—Psalms 119:28

So, it has come to this—even after all your prayers and efforts to restore your marriage—your wife tells you it is over; she wants a divorce. Indeed, your soul is weary with sorrow.

You still love your wife, so do you hang on to hope or do you finally let go? If you have children in the home, what does this mean for them? How will it affect the time you spend with your kids? There are no easy answers to these questions.

But there are easy answers to how to address the following questions: Is the enemy inciting you to anger toward God for not rewarding your faithfulness to Him and to your wife, as well as your diligent trusting Him with your marriage? Is the devil nudging you to speak words of criticism toward and about your wife?

Although you cannot control your wife's decisions, you do have power over Satan with your words and behaviors—with God as your defender. As the Lord strengthens you according to His Word, you will thwart the devil's attempts to completely demolish what you have in Christ, and what your children see in you. In this you will be more than a conqueror. Yay and Amen!

What do you need to do to avoid letting your spiritual guard down?

Week 50 Reflections

Day 1: This week's verse in full, or a portion thereof:

____

Day 2: This verse empowers me to:

____

Day 3: My response to the entreaty at the end of the message:

____

Day 4: What I most appreciate about my wife this day/week:

____

Day 5: Prayer:

____

Week 51   When your wife denounces Christ . . .

"To the rest I say this (I, not the Lord): If any brother has a wife who is not a believer and she is willing to live with him, he must not divorce her."—1 Corinthians 7:12

How heart-rending it is when your spouse, who once claimed Jesus as her Savior, now rejects Him. How could she who knew Christ personally disown Him? Yet, Paul recognized it happens— "If we disown him, he will also disown us;" (2 Timothy 2:12). Knowing the woman you love is now disowned by God must cause you excruciating pain, especially if she continues living with you.

"But if the unbeliever leaves, let it be so. The brother or sister is not bound in such circumstances; God has called us to live in peace." (1 Corinthians 7:15)

Yes, Father God has called you to live in peace—peace that passes all understanding. "Do not be anxious about anything, but in every situation, by prayer and petition, with thanksgiving, present your requests to God. And the peace of God, which transcends all understanding, will guard your hearts and your minds in Christ Jesus. Finally, brothers and sisters, whatever is true, whatever is noble, whatever is right, whatever is pure, whatever is lovely, whatever is admirable—if anything is excellent or praiseworthy—*think about such things*. Whatever you have learned or received or heard from me, or seen in me—

put it into practice. And the God of peace will be with you."
(Philippians 4:6-9)

Will you think about these things?

Week 51 Reflections

Day 1: This week's verse in full, or a portion thereof:

____

____

____

Day 2: This verse empowers me to:

____

____

____

Day 3: My response to the entreaty at the end of the message:

____

____

____

Day 4: What I most appreciate about my wife this day/week:

____

____

____

Day 5: Prayer:

____

____

____

167

Week 52   When your wife is abusive/violent . . .

"If it is possible, as far as it depends on you, live at peace with everyone. Do not take revenge, my dear friends, but leave room for God's wrath, for it is written: 'It is mine to avenge; I will repay,' says the Lord."—Romans 12:18-20

You love your wife . . . just not the way she treats you. But, you say in defense of her, "Most of the time she's good to me. She doesn't always hurt me. And afterwards she apologizes and promises to never do it again."

Perhaps you haven't told anyone of this abuse because you don't want others to judge you or her. You may fear your pastor and other Christians will insist you stay in this relationship. So you endure and "turn the other cheek." Isn't that what the Bible says to do?

God's Word also says "He will rescue them from oppression and violence, for precious is their blood in his sight." (Psalm 72:14)

The truth of the matter is, no matter what *you* do to live at peace with your spouse, it doesn't stop the violence. So it is *not possible* to safely live in your home.

Safety is an absolute must!

Pray! Call the National Domestic Violence Hotline: 1-800-799-7233

This hotline is open 24/7 in English and Spanish, plus 200 more languages through interpretation service.

Don't wait until it is too late.

How can you be strong and take the right steps?

Week 52 Reflections

Day 1: This week's verse in full, or a portion thereof:

____

____

____

Day 2: This verse empowers me to:

____

____

____

Day 3: My response to the entreaty at the end of the message:

____

____

____

Day 4: What I most appreciate about my wife this day/week:

____

____

____

Day 5: Prayer:

____

____

____

About the Author

Mary Stone, a follower of Christ and lover of God's Word, is devoted to sharing the wisdom and encouragement she has gleaned over the many years she has studied the Bible and worked in the field of Counseling. Her mission is threefold: for God to get the glory, for readers to get victory, and for Satan to be defeated.

Mary is an inspiring keynote speaker and author, who writes with openness and sincerity. She began her career in higher education after earning a Master's Degree in Counseling at the University of Nebraska, Kearney. In 2011, Lower Columbia College in Longview, Washington conferred upon her Faculty Emeritus for her years of outstanding and dedicated service. In addition to her career as a college Counselor, Mary practiced as a Licensed Mental Health Therapist for many years.

The author's first published non-fiction book, *Run in the Path of Peace—the Secret of Being Content No Matter What*, continues to garner her speaking engagements at Christian conferences, book groups, and virtual conversations. Visit Amazon.com to order *Run in the Path of Peace* in paperback or ebook.

Mary loves to write, garden, travel, do puzzles, and spend time with her family—not necessarily in that order, depending on the day and on the Pacific Northwest weather.

She and her husband make their home in Washington state.

Mary invites you to contact her at:

maryellenstone@hotmail.com

and/or subscribe to her monthly devotional blog, *Sowing Seeds*,

at:

https://marystonewriter.com

www.ingramcontent.com/pod-product-compliance
Lightning Source LLC
Chambersburg PA
CBHW071745150726
47998CB00005B/1807